This book belongs to

....

Written by Tim Bugbird.
Illustrated by Stuart Lynch.
Designed by Karen Morrison.

The Fox Factor

Tim Bugbird • Stuart Lynch

make
believe
ideas

Fabio Fox loved to **sing**; he sang wherever he could:

in the **bath,**

on his **bike**

and even in **bed,**

but really he **wasn't much good!**

COTTON WOOL

He sang for his friends, if asked to **or not,**
and here's the funniest thing:
whatever they said went
into his head as . . .

"That was
a-ma-zing!"

Every night, he had the same **dream** —
fame would knock on his door!
But **every day,** he'd wake to find
things as they were before.

Then, one day,
he saw a **sign.**
It said:
"COME TO OUR AUDITIONS!"

"I've got the
fox factor!"
Fabio thought.
"I'll win and fulfil
my **ambitions."**

Fabio stood still while the judges looked stern, and asked,

"What song will you do?"

THE JUDGES

He said,

"Wash your Socks, Stinky Fox."

Then created a

hullabaloo!

The audience was lost for words — his performance was so **bizarre!**

A **million** views made Fabio Fox

an overnight

internet star!

Finally **famous,** Fabio's life changed in fabulous ways.
Glitz and glamour **24/7,** this was a typical day:

Wake up and have
a relaxing bubble bath

Posh breakfast
of French toast
squares on sticks

Luxury spa session,
including brush,
tint and curl

Photo shoot for a fancy magazine

Be chased by paparazzi while just trying to lead a normal life

Posh dinner of fried eggs shaped like stars

And to make sure he always arrived on time (or was it just to be seen?), with 16 seats and a Jacuzzi, he hired a **stretch limousine!**

Fabio's life soon **became** all he **dreamt** it would be.

He was given a recording contract – **"Stinky Fox"** was out on **CD!**

At a party in his **new penthouse,** Fabio took to the **floor,** surrounded by his fancy, **new friends** — his old ones were **stopped** at the door.

This should have been
Fabio's moment —
a superstar truly born.
But remember, Fabio **could not sing** —
he **honked** like an old **foghorn.**

Watching Fabio **dance** on stage
was **always** lots of fun.
But who would buy his music?
Every note hit was a **bum!**

The DJs said,
"We can't play that!
We're sorry if this
sounds **rude."**

"But it'll give our

listeners **earache**

and none of us

wants to be **sued!"**

Stinky Fox was **Flop of the Year**;
Fabio's fame was at an **end**.
He threw a party to **cheer** himself up,
inviting his **VIP** friends.

But everyone was **too busy**;
no one could make the trip.
So Fabio had a party for **one**,
alone with his chip-'n'-dip.

They took back Fabio's **limo** and the **keys** to his penthouse pad.

This was now Fabio's **typical** day –
grey and a little bit sad:

Wake up and fall back
to sleep for an hour

Boring breakfast
of very dull toast

Nothing

Ordinary lunch of boring,
circle-shaped carrots

More nothing

Dull dinner, including
something too dull
even to mention

But, though he
didn't know it,
all was far from lost.
His story took
another twist,
now he'd learnt what
fame had **cost** . . . .

Walking through the streets, one night,

Fabio heard a **familiar sound.**

He followed the noise through the alleys

and **look** who he finally found!

His old friends were dancing to **"Stinky Fox"** –

what a **terrible** din!

"We made up this dance to remember you.

We found your CD **in a bin!**"

Fabio saw he'd been a fool.
"I won **fame,** but lost my **friends** —
I forgot what really mattered.
How can I make **amends?**"

His **friends** said they would have to think,
but it didn't take them long:
they asked Fabio Fox to join them
in **remaking** his terrible song.

The friends all worked **together**, each doing what they did **best**.

The song now sounded much **better**,
but who could have guessed the rest?

Their group became a worldwide smash:

Fabio's Famous Crew!

And Fabio learnt that with **friends** by your side,
dreams really can **come** true.